A GO-Kart at School

written by Jay Dale

May 9th

Dear Principal Ritter,

My name is Clare Ling,
and I really love go-kart racing.
I race my go-kart every weekend.
My dad always comes with me.
Go-kart racing is lots of fun,
and it is a great sport.

This is a *photo* of Dad
and me at the go-kart track.

Here is a photo of me during my last race.

This letter is to ask you if my dad can bring my go-kart to school.

I would like the children in my class to try go-karting. Then they can see how much fun it can be.

I started racing go-karts when I was eight years old.
My dad is a really good teacher.
He tells me everything I need to know
about go-kart racing.
It's hard at the start but once you learn
how to *drive* a go-kart, it's easy.

It would be really great if the children in my class
could have a ride in my go-kart.
I know all the moms and dads
would think it is a great idea.
They could come and watch, too.

It would be great fun for me to show the other children why I love go-kart racing.

Some children have their own go-karts.

My dad can bring my go-kart to school any day.
Dad works from home, so it's easy for him
to come to school during the day.

I thought the best place to try out my go-kart
would be on the *sports field*.
There is a *track* around the outside of the sports field
that would be just right for a go-kart.
Also, the sports field is a long way
from the school *buildings*.
Go-karts can make lots of *noise*!

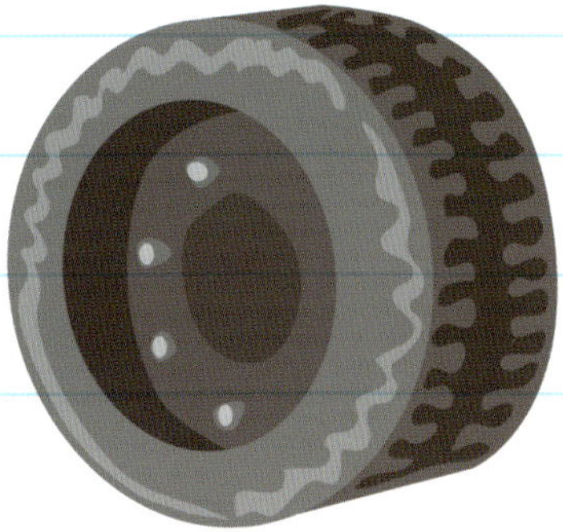

This picture shows the track around the sports field.

Lots of children love go-karting.

When I race my go-kart, it is very important that I wear special *clothes*.
I also wear a special *helmet* and *gloves*.
They keep me safe.

My dad can bring some special clothes, helmets, and gloves for the other children.
That way, they will be safe, too.

Some of the moms, dads, and teachers could help the children get into the special clothes.
That way, they will be ready when it's their turn.

Go-kart Clothes

I hope you think it is a really good idea for my dad to bring my go-kart to school.

There are many great things about racing go-karts.

1. You learn the *road rules*.
2. You learn how to *steer*.
3. You learn a lot about go-kart *engines*.
4. You have lots of fun.
5. You make lots of friends.

This boy is learning how to steer.

This is a photo of my friend, Ashton.

Go-kart racing is a great sport.
It would be fun for the children in my class to learn something new.
And maybe some of the children will come to my go-karting club with me.

Look at the *tires*.
They keep us safe.

Every go-kart has a number.

Some go-karts go very fast.

I really hope I can bring my go-kart to school.
Thank you for looking at my letter.
I hope you think my idea is a good one.

From,
Clare Ling

Dad took this photo last week at the track.

Picture Glossary

buildings

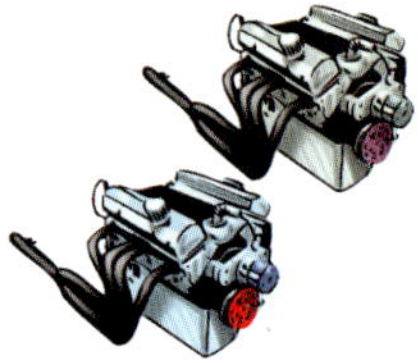

engines

noise

sports field

clothes

gloves

photo

tires

drive/steer

helmet

road rules

track